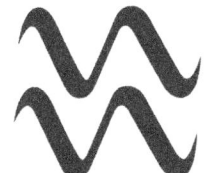

2023
2044

Pluto in Aquarius

2023 - 2044

AN IN-DEPTH EXPLORATION
OF THE ASTROLOGICAL TRANSIT

Ω

OMEGA TEAM

Star greetings, mate!

"This book really dives into what Pluto moving through Aquarius means and how it's affecting things. It's a big deal in astrology right now.

And hey, it's not just some regular read. It's like a roadmap for figuring out how the stars are shaking up our world and getting us ready for whatever's coming our way."

PART I
" A Historical Perspective of Pluto in Aquarius "
[1532-1553] [1777-1798] [2023-2044]

PART II
" When Power Becomes Collective and Technological.
The Transition from Vertical to Horizontal Power.
Unleashing Disruption and Redefining Success."

PART III
Revelation, Revolution and Renaissance:
Dismantling Old Paradigms and Building New Futures

APPENDIX I
Sign-by-Sign Forecast
of Pluto Transit in Aquarius.

APPENDIX II
Meanings of Pluto in
the 12 Astrological Houses.

PART I

" A Historical Perspective of Pluto in Aquarius "

[1532-1553] [1777-1798] [2023-2044]

A historical perspective of Pluto in Aquarius

Pluto's transit through Aquarius has historically been a period of great scientific, technological and social upheavals, with both transformative and destructive potentials. We are going to analyze the two previous transits and an estimate of what the one that began in 2023 may be like.

1532-1553
The dissemination of knowledge and challenges to authority

Between 1532 and 1553, we lived through a crucial period. It was an era in which Europe experienced an explosion of knowledge, driven in large part by the spread of the printing press. Although the invention of the printing press occurred before this period, it was during these years that there was a significant increase in the number of books printed in Europe. In 1500, only two million books were printed in Europe, but by 1550, that number had skyrocketed to 20 million. This increase in the availability of books and pamphlets facilitated the spread of knowledge and ideas, impacting everything from religious literature to scientific treatises and political pamphlets.

One of the most important milestones of this period was the publication of *"On the Revolutions of the Celestial Spheres"* by Nicholas Copernicus in 1543. In this book, Copernicus argued that the Sun was the center of the solar system rather than the Earth, challenging thus the previous cosmological conceptions. Although his work marked the beginning of the Copernican Revolution and laid the foundation for the Scientific Revolution, he was initially resisted and his book was even banned by the Church.

The Church also attempted to control the spread of information by creating lists of banned books and censoring works deemed inappropriate. This period also saw the Protestant Reformation, which weakened the authority of the Catholic Church and fostered an environment more conducive to scientific debate.

In addition to these scientific and social developments, this period was also marked by imperial exploration and expansion.

In summary, Pluto's transit through Aquarius between 1532 and 1553 was a period of radical change, characterized by scientific advances, religious struggles, and imperial exploration. These events laid the foundation for the modern era and had a lasting impact on Western society and culture.

1777-1798
The Age of Revolutions: Scientific, Political and Technological Advances

The period from 1777 to 1798 was a time of transformation, marked by important astronomical, political and technological developments. At the beginning of this era of Pluto in Aquarius, in 1781, astronomer William Herschel made a momentous discovery: he found the planet Uranus, expanding humanity's understanding of the solar system. This was a turning point not only for astronomy, but also for astrology, as it added a new celestial body to the known planets.

Simultaneously, the American Revolution was developing, with the 13 American colonies declaring independence from Great Britain and establishing the

United States of America. Interestingly, while the United States is commonly associated with Pluto in Capricorn, much of the fundamental governmental structure with its system of checks and balances was actually established during the final stages of Pluto's transit through Aquarius. This suggests that there was something about democratic principles and attempts to establish a system of balanced power that bore the stamp of Pluto in Aquarius.

Across the Atlantic, the French Revolution was also unfolding, marked by the overthrow of the French monarchy and a period of radical political and social upheaval. This included the Reign of Terror, where thousands were executed by guillotine due to widespread paranoia and suspicion of traitors. Interestingly, the left-right political divide that still prevails today emerged from the factions that formed in the French National Assembly during this tumultuous period.

Alongside these political revolutions, the era also saw an explosion of technological innovations. The steam engine, developed by James Watt, helped fuel the Industrial Revolution and transform manufacturing. Advances in textile production, such as the *spinning jenny* and the power loom, significantly increased efficiency and output. Additionally, key inventions such as the battery, by Alessandro Volta, and the first smallpox vaccine, by Edward Jenner, made important contributions to science and medicine.

One of the most captivating technological advances of the era was the Montgolfier brothers' pioneering work on hot air balloons. Its historic first manned flight in 1783 captured the public's imagination and laid the foundation for future aviation. Interestingly, the Montgolfiers' background in paper-making and experimentation with different materials, including silk, contributed to their success in developing this new mode of flight.

During this period of Pluto in Aquarius, writer Mary Shelley, born with Pluto conjunct her Midheaven in Aquarius, wrote the iconic science fiction novel Frankenstein. The story serves as a warning about the potential dangers of unbridled scientific ambition and the consequences of "playing God" by creating artificial life. Shelley's own tragic personal life, marked by the loss of her mother and other loved ones, likely influenced the themes of her work.

Along with Shelley's Frankenstein, another notable figure of the time was Napoleon Bonaparte. As a young Corsican sent to France during Pluto's entry into Aquarius, Napoleon's rise to power and subsequent transformation into an autocratic ruler provides an interesting counterpoint to the democratic ideals that were emerging during this period. Napoleon's military successes and his eventual coronation as Emperor illustrate the tensions between democracy and authoritarianism that can arise during Pluto's transit of Aquarius.

Interestingly, the Haitian Revolution, led by Toussaint L'Ouverture, also took place during this era of Pluto in Aquarius. As the first and only successful slave rebellion that resulted in the establishment of an independent nation, the Haitian Revolution was a powerful expression of the democratic principles that were being advocated elsewhere, but with the added dimension of racial and social justice.

Overall, the Pluto in Aquarius period from 1777 to 1798 was a time of profound transformation, marked by scientific, technological, and political revolutions that laid the foundations of the modern world. While the period saw the rise of democratic ideals and attempts to establish balanced systems of power, it also highlighted the potential for those ideals to be subverted or co-opted by autocratic figures such as Napoleon. The ethical dilemmas posed by rapid technological progress, as exemplified in Mary Shelley's Frankenstein, also foreshadowed challenges that would continue to arise in the centuries to come.

Outlook for the Future
2023-2044

I

Pluto made its first entry into Aquarius in 2023 and after several retrogradations towards Capricorn, it will remain in the sign of Aquarius until 2044, which marks the beginning of a new period of Pluto in Aquarius. This leads us to reflect on the recurring trends and themes we have seen in previous Pluto in Aquarius periods throughout history.

One of the key themes is the use of technological advances to gain power and control. Technology, knowledge and information have proven to have great transformative power over society. We saw examples of how developments like the printing press, gunpowder, and cotton had a profound impact.

Another recurring theme is the transfer of technology from foreign or "alien" cultures, which has had a transformative effect on society, politics and power. From the adoption of gunpowder from China to the development of silk, these technological exchanges have been catalysts for significant change.

The idea of the "foreign" or "alien" also seems to be gaining relevance, not only in terms of artificial intelligence and the possible creation of a new *sentient species* on Earth, but also in relation to the discovery of extraterrestrial life forms, even at the microbial level. This could have a revolutionary impact on our conception of ourselves and our place in the universe, similar to the Copernican revolution.

China's role has also been a recurring theme, and it is notable that its rise as a global superpower occurred just before Pluto's entry into Aquarius. This raises questions about tensions between China and other world powers, especially the United States, over technologies and other areas.

Another prominent theme is the tension between democracy and autocracy, and how autocratic leaders can attempt to establish control through the illusion of democracy.

Finally, technological advances, especially in areas such as artificial intelligence, are anticipated to have a transformative impact on society, similar to how paper and the printing press affected the spread of ideas in the past. This could mark a turning point in history, comparable to the transition from the 19th to the 20th century.

II

Pluto's entry into Aquarius will bring a mix of technological advances, attempts to control information and technology, and tensions between democracy and autocracy. One of the main issues will be the difficulty in distinguishing between what was generated by AI and what was produced by humans. This will pose challenges, such as the possibility of wedding photos of the future being taken in AI-generated simulations.

Another important issue will be attempts by governments and large entities to control the flow of information, similar to the Church's list of banned books in the past. Although these attempts at censorship may be temporarily successful, the truth will eventually prevail, as it did with the discoveries of Copernicus. This could also apply to topics like astrology, which has recently seen a resurgence in popularity.

Another aspect will be espionage and attempts to monopolize key technologies, such as computer chips, microprocessors and artificial intelligence. Whoever controls these technologies will have enormous power and influence on a global level. In addition, we will see how old technologies are merged and refined to create new weapons of war, such as drones, robots, AI, lasers and cyber warfare, which raises serious ethical implications, such as whether autonomous machines should be allowed to make decisions. kill humans without human supervision.

Another theme will be the experience of scientists who create something for the love of science, but then see it used for destructive purposes, similar to the story of Frankenstein. This raises questions about the responsibilities and potential dangers of pushing the boundaries of knowledge.

The development of the scientific method and experimentation will be important topics during this period. There will also be tensions between democracy and authoritarianism, with autocratic leaders attempting to establish control through the illusion of democracy.

Furthermore, we are likely to see events that cause an irreversible change in intellectual and social trends. The COVID-19 pandemic showed that we are still vulnerable to these types of events, which could be a harbinger of what is to come.

Flight will also be a significant topic, with the development of commercial space flight and possibly even small-scale local flight, such as drones that can carry people. This will be reinforced by the entry of Uranus into Gemini, another sign related to transportation.

Finally, there will be tensions with globalization, with some countries attempting to bring production of certain goods back to their own countries, partly in reaction to the vulnerabilities exposed by the pandemic. This could mark a setback in the globalized and interconnected world order that seemed inevitable until recently.

III

The current trend appears to be toward deglobalization and the decline of the United States' global influence. This is partly because the previous global order was linked to the Cold War, when the United States used its naval fleet to keep trade routes safe in exchange for other countries not becoming communist. That agreement is no longer in effect and the United States no longer has the same interest in patrolling the oceans.

This could lead to a more multipolar world, with a greater distribution of power rather than a single dominant superpower. This is symbolically related to the transit of Pluto through Aquarius, a more social sign where power is distributed more equitably. However, it is unclear whether current superpowers such as China and Russia will have the ability to maintain their status in the future, so new global leaders could emerge.

An important aspect is that human progress has been driven by socialization and the exchange of information between different places. This relates to the social nature of Aquarius. Hyperconnection through the Internet could further accelerate this scientific and technological progress, but it also carries risks and challenges.

Another relevant point is that Pluto in Aquarius will oppose the Pluto in Leo generation, which includes the Baby Boomers born in the 40s and 50s. This will likely mark the end of that generation's power and influence.

Finally, it is worth mentioning that the development of artificial intelligence has led to humans learning from the perceptions and capabilities of machines. This suggests that in this era, humans could learn from artificial intelligence or extraterrestrials, which could provide important insights.

Overall, an era of profound change and innovation, with risks and opportunities, is anticipated as the current global order is transformed.

PART II

" **When Power Becomes Collective and Technological.**
The Transition from Vertical to Horizontal Power.
Unleashing Disruption and Redefining Success."

Pluto's entry into Aquarius

Pluto, the planet that represents power, transformation and regeneration, has been transiting the sign of Capricorn since 2008. During these 15 years, we have witnessed profound changes in power structures, institutions and practices that previously They considered themselves unbreakable. Now, in 2023, Pluto is preparing to enter the sign of Aquarius, which will undoubtedly mark a new era.

Although Pluto briefly visited Aquarius in late March and mid-June 2023, its final entry into this sign will occur on November 19, 2024, where it will remain for the next 20 years. This transit represents a crucial moment, since Pluto, the planet of power, is now in the sign of Aquarius, the sign of innovation, technology and vision of the future.

During this brief period of testing, we have been able to glimpse some of the manifestations of Pluto in Aquarius. One of the most obvious has been the aesthetic of chaos, where we see influencers and ordinary people showing disordered spaces and accumulation, as opposed to the perfection and order that used to predominate. This reflects how Pluto in Aquarius is challenging established standards and making visible the need for flexibility and adaptation.

Likewise, we have witnessed a bombardment of information and debates around artificial intelligence and its impact on the world of work. Concern about the possible substitution of jobs by AI has been a recurring theme, leading to demands and negotiations by workers, as in the case of the Hollywood writers and actors strike.

These early manifestations of Pluto in Aquarius give us a glimpse of what is to come. Power, technology and vision for the future intertwine, challenging structures and practices previously considered immovable. It is important to note that these changes are not exclusively due to the entry of Pluto into Aquarius, but are part of a broader transformation process that has been underway in recent years.

However, it is undeniable that the presence of Pluto in Aquarius will accelerate and make these processes of change even more visible. At a collective level, we will see a transition from the power of the elite, represented by Pluto in Capricorn, towards a more distributed and technological power, typical of Pluto in Aquarius. This will be reflected in areas such as politics, education, business and group dynamics.

It is important to keep in mind that this transit of Pluto will not be a simple process or free of resistance. Fixed signs, like Aquarius, often have difficulty embracing change quickly and radically. Therefore, we are likely to see tensions and conflicts as this power transition occurs.

In summary, the entry of Pluto into Aquarius marks a momentous moment in the history of humanity. This transit invites us to question and rethink power structures, technology and the vision of the future, opening the door to a deep and lasting transformation in all areas of our society.

The manifestations of Pluto in Aquarius

Since Pluto made its brief foray into Aquarius in late March and mid-June 2023, we have been able to observe some of the ways this powerful planet is beginning to shape our collective. One of the most obvious manifestations has been the aesthetics of chaos that has emerged on social networks and in the daily lives of many people.

Influencers and ordinary users have begun to share images and videos of their personal spaces, showing an apparent disorder that contrasts with the perfection and minimalism that used to predominate. This aesthetic reflects a liberation from the rigid expectations and standards that used to govern our environments. Pluto in Aquarius seems to be challenging the need for control and order, inviting us to embrace fluidity and authenticity.

Another notable manifestation has been the bombardment of information and debates around artificial intelligence and its impact on the world of work.
This focus on AI and its role in the future of employment is a reflection of how Pluto in Aquarius is making visible the challenges and opportunities that arise from technology. The need to adapt and rethink our careers and skills has become increasingly pressing, as automation and technological innovation transform the employment landscape.

Beyond these examples, it is important to highlight that the manifestations of Pluto in Aquarius go far beyond what we can observe on the surface. This transit is challenging the narratives and structures we have taken for granted for decades, inviting us to question and rethink the way we organize our society, our institutions, and our forms of leadership.

As Pluto continues its journey through Aquarius, we are likely to see an acceleration of these transformation processes, with disruptive changes in areas such as politics, education, and group dynamics. Technology, innovation and a vision of the future will become fundamental pillars of this new era, challenging traditional models and opening the door to new possibilities.

The legacy of Pluto in Capricorn

Before delving into the implications of Pluto in Aquarius, it is important to reflect on the legacy that this planet has left during its transit through the sign of Capricorn, which lasted almost 15 years, from 2008 to 2023.

During this period, Pluto in Capricorn has witnessed and catalyzed profound changes in power structures, institutions, and practices previously considered unbreakable. We have witnessed the erosion of trust in traditional authorities, as well as the growing questioning of the models of success and personal fulfillment that used to be the norm.

The Pluto in Capricorn narrative has been marked by an obsession with success, money and power. We have seen how this energy has driven people to pursue goals and achievements at all costs, often at the expense of their well-being and their connection to what is essential. Social networks have been a clear reflection of this trend, with constant messages of "never stop" and "goals first."

However, this legacy has also brought with it some positive aspects. Pluto in Capricorn has challenged the notion that there is only one path to success, opening the door to new forms of entrepreneurship and personal fulfillment. We have witnessed the emergence of disruptive careers and professions, which challenge traditional models and better adapt to the changing needs of society.

Furthermore, Pluto in Capricorn has highlighted the need to question and transform the power structures that have dominated for decades. The accumulation of power in the hands of an elite has been questioned, and the door has been opened to greater transparency and a more equitable distribution of power.

Now, with Pluto in Aquarius, we are entering a new era where power, technology and vision are intertwined in a more dynamic and collaborative way. This transit represents an opportunity to build on the foundations that Pluto in Capricorn has established, and to imagine and materialize new forms of social, economic and political organization.

It is important to recognize that Pluto's legacy in Capricorn will not completely disappear with its entry into Aquarius. There will be a transition and coexistence of both energies, which will generate tensions and resistance to change. However, this period of transformation also gives us the opportunity to integrate the best of both worlds, creating a balance between structure and innovation, between power and collaboration.

The transition of power from Capricorn to Aquarius

As Pluto leaves the sign of Capricorn and moves into Aquarius, we are witnessing a fundamental transition in power dynamics on a collective level. This paradigm shift represents a challenge and an opportunity to rethink the way power is exercised and distributed in our society.

Under the influence of Pluto in Capricorn, power was concentrated in the hands of an elite, in hierarchical structures and in traditional institutions. It was a vertical power model, where decisions and authority were imposed from above, leaving little room for participation and collaboration. This narrative has been reflected in various areas, from the corporate world to politics.

However, with the entry of Pluto into Aquarius, we are witnessing a change in the way power is conceived and exercised. Aquarius, the sign of innovation, technology and vision for the future, is driving a transition towards a more horizontal, more distributed and more collaborative power model.

In this new paradigm, power is no longer concentrated in an elite, but is dispersed and shared among different actors. Group dynamics and collaboration networks take on fundamental importance, challenging traditional hierarchical structures. Decision-making becomes more transparent and participatory, with greater exchange of ideas and openness to innovation.

This transition of power is also reflected in areas such as education and the world of work. Pluto in Aquarius questions the rigidity of traditional curricula and training models, advocating for greater adaptability and relevance based on the changing needs of society. Likewise, the world of work is undergoing a transformation, with the emergence of new careers and forms of employment that challenge traditional schemes.

It is important to highlight that this transition of power will not be a simple process nor free of resistance. Therefore, we are likely to see tensions and conflicts as this transition occurs, with those clinging to established power models and those embracing new forms of leadership and organization.

Pluto in Aquarius invites us to rethink the way we conceive and exercise power, opening the door to greater participation, transparency and collective responsibility.

Aquarius Predominant People

As Pluto enters the sign of Aquarius, it is important to pay special attention to how this transit will affect people who have a strong Aquarius presence in their birth charts, whether in the sun, ascendant, or moon.

These people, who tend to be naturally curious, innovative, and future-oriented, will be particularly impacted by Pluto's entry into their sign. For them, this transit represents an opportunity to deeply question and rethink their beliefs, their goals, and their place in the world.

One of the most notable characteristics of Aquarius-dominant people is their tendency to question authority and established structures. With Pluto in your sign, this inclination will be even more accentuated, leading you to further challenge narratives and practices that were previously considered set in stone.

This can generate great restlessness in them and a feeling of being at a turning point in their lives. Questions like "Where am I going?" and "What will I do with my life?" They may emerge with greater intensity, prompting them to seek new forms of expression and personal fulfillment.

Additionally, people with predominant Aquarius tend to have a broad and visionary view of the world. With Pluto in their sign, this ability to imagine and project the future will be enhanced, which can lead them to embrace changes and make bold decisions that challenge traditional models.

It will be crucial for these people to develop the ability to balance their desire for innovation and freedom with the need to maintain some structure and stability in their lives. Finding this balance will allow you to make the most of the opportunities that Pluto in Aquarius offers you, without falling into paralysis or frustration.

In short, Aquarius-dominant people will be deeply impacted by Pluto's entry into their sign. This transit will offer you the opportunity to question, transform and reinvent yourself, but it will also require great flexibility and adaptability to navigate these times of change.

Resistance to change and necessary adaptation

While Pluto's entry into Aquarius represents an opportunity for transformation and innovation, it is important to recognize that this transit will not be without resistance and challenges. After all, change rarely comes smoothly and without obstacles.

One of the main sources of resistance may come from those people and structures that have clung to Pluto in Capricorn's patterns of power and organization. These individuals and systems have become accustomed to verticality, rigidity and concentration of authority, and may feel their position threatened by the arrival of Pluto in Aquarius.

Thus, we are likely to see a struggle to maintain the *status quo*, with attempts to cling to old ways of doing things. This can manifest itself in various areas, from politics and institutions to group dynamics and personal relationships.

To successfully navigate this transition period, developing resilience and flexibility will be crucial. Both individually and collectively, we will need to be open to rethinking our beliefs, our structures and our ways of relating.

This will involve a process of detachment and openness to the new, which can be uncomfortable and challenging for many. However, it is in this ability to let go of the known and embrace the unknown where lies the key to making the most of the opportunities that Pluto in Aquarius offers us.

Likewise, it will be important to cultivate patience and understanding. Recognizing that change does not happen overnight, and that there will be moments of tension and conflict, will help us navigate this period of transition more calmly.

Ultimately, Pluto's entry into Aquarius challenges us to rethink our ways of organizing, leading, and collaborating. This will require a collective effort, in which each of us must take an active role in building a more equitable, innovative future adapted to the needs of society.

A look into the future

As Pluto settles into Aquarius, we are facing a defining moment in human history. This planetary transit represents a unique opportunity to reimagine and reconfigure the way we conceive and exercise power, technology, and vision.

Under the influence of Pluto in Aquarius, we are called to transcend traditional models of leadership and social organization. Instead of a concentration of power in the hands of an elite, Pluto in Aquarius invites us to adopt more collaborative, transparent and decentralized approaches.

This transition will be reflected in various areas, from politics and economics to education and group dynamics. We will see how hierarchical and rigid structures give way to more flexible forms of organization, where participation, the exchange of ideas and innovation take on a central role.

Likewise, technology and artificial intelligence will become tools increasingly integrated into our lives. However, under the influence of this planet, its development and application will be increasingly oriented towards the common good and the improvement of the human condition.

In this sense, Pluto in Aquarius challenges us to rethink the way we conceive progress and success. It will no longer be enough to pursue individual goals or accumulate power and wealth at all costs. Instead, a more holistic vision will be required, one that balances personal needs with those of the collective and prioritizes long-term sustainability and well-being.

This transit of Pluto will have a profound impact on the way we relate and organize ourselves as a society. Group dynamics will transform, giving way to greater collaboration, exchange of ideas and shared decision making. Education, for its part, must adapt to prepare new generations for the challenges and opportunities that lie ahead.

Although this process of change will not be free of resistance and tensions, the entry of Pluto into Aquarius represents a unique opportunity to build a more equitable, innovative future adapted to the needs of humanity. It will be up to us, as individuals and as a collective, to embrace this transition with an open, flexible mindset committed to transformation.

PART III

Revelation, Revolution and Renaissance:

Dismantling Old Paradigms
and Building New Futures

The entry of Pluto into the sign of Aquarius marks the beginning of a time of profound changes and radical transformations on a global level. This planetary transit represents a historical moment of great significance, in which a wave of subversion and rebirth will be unleashed that will shake the foundations of our societies. Pluto, the planet associated with destruction and regeneration, will reach the sign of innovation and vision of the future, revealing the weaknesses inherent in the systems and power structures that have dominated until now. This "Plutonian storm" will expose the corruption and abuses of the elites, challenging the established order and opening the way to the emergence of new forms of organization and collective action. In this context of disruption and change, we will witness revolutions in the technological, economic and social spheres, which will completely reconfigure the global panorama. From the decline of traditional television to the diversification of the human species, the era of Pluto in Aquarius will lead us towards the construction of new paradigms and more just, equitable and sustainable futures.

This process of revelation, revolution and rebirth represents both an opportunity and a challenge for humanity. As old power structures crumble, space opens up for collective reinvention and profound transformation of our societies.

The entry of Pluto into Aquarius and its historical significance

The entry of Pluto into the sign of Aquarius is an astrological event of great significance, which marks the beginning of a new era of profound changes and radical transformations on a global level. Pluto, the planet that represents subversion, destruction and regeneration, now enters the revolutionary sign of Aquarius, bringing with it the potential to dismantle old paradigms and usher in a renewed vision of the future.

This Pluto transition, which occurs approximately every 240 years, is a historical moment of great importance, as it usually coincides with periods of profound social, political and cultural transformations. As happened with the entry of Pluto into Capricorn, which preceded events such as the 2008 financial crisis and the rise of disruptive social and political movements, the arrival of Pluto in Aquarius portends a new cycle of radical changes.

Aquarius, the sign of innovation, technology and vision of the future, now becomes the stage where Pluto will deploy its transformative power. This transition marks the beginning of a revolutionary era, in which old social models and paradigms will be questioned and challenged, giving way to the emergence of new forms of organization, collective action and exercise of power.

The entry of Pluto into Aquarius occurs at a time of great astrological effervescence, with the conjunction of Jupiter and Saturn in this same sign at the end of 2020, which has further accelerated the transition process towards the Age of Aquarius.

During the 20 years that Pluto will remain in Aquarius, we will witness profound transformations in the way power is exercised on a global level. Great powers and traditional geopolitical systems will be challenged by new factors, such as technology, artificial intelligence and cyberwarfare, which will alter the established balance of forces. Likewise, we will witness the emergence of new social classes and organizational models that will question the current systems of political representation, advocating for more participatory and horizontal forms of decision-making.

In summary, the entry of Pluto into Aquarius marks the beginning of an era of transcendental changes, in which old structures and paradigms will be dismantled to make way for a renewed vision of the future. This planetary transit represents a unique opportunity for the transformation and reinvention of our societies, but it also entails challenges and turbulence that we must face with courage and determination.

Subversion and change of the established order

The arrival of Pluto in the sign of Aquarius marks the beginning of a period of profound subversion and questioning of the established order. As a planet that represents transformation at a deep level, Pluto has the ability to dismantle and expose the weaknesses inherent in the systems and power structures that have dominated our societies.

One of the main effects of Pluto in Aquarius will be the revelation of the shames and abuses committed by elites, governments, large institutions and corporations. What was kept hidden or covered up under layers of privilege and opacity will come to light, exposing the corruption, exploitation and lack of integrity that have characterized the exercise of power in recent decades.

Just as Pluto in Capricorn revealed the vulnerabilities of the global financial system, the entry of this planet into Aquarius will bring to light the deficiencies and abuses of the systems of power that have dominated the public and political sphere. From governments and institutions to large technology and media companies, nothing will be safe from the scrutinizing gaze of Pluto, which will be in charge of exposing their shame and weaknesses.

This process of revealing and dismantling power structures will have a profound impact on the way authority and decision-making are exercised globally. Pluto in Aquarius will bring with it a radical reconfiguration of geopolitical balances, challenging traditional models based on the division of borders, zones of influence and power blocks.

In their place, new ways of exercising power will emerge, more in line with the Aquarian vision of global interconnection and cooperation between peoples and nations. Factors such as technology, artificial intelligence, cyberwarfare and information manipulation will become crucially important in redefining power relations on a global scale.

Far from being a linear and predictable process, the entry of Pluto into Aquarius will be characterized by great volatility and effervescence. We will witness a succession of disruptive events, crises and conflicts that will shake the foundations of the current political, economic and social systems. This turbulence, although it can generate uncertainty and unrest, also opens the door to the emergence of new paradigms and forms of organization more in line with the needs and aspirations of humanity in the coming era.

Revelation of weaknesses in power systems and structures

This exposure of the weaknesses and vices of elites and power centers will have a profound impact on the trust and legitimacy of traditional governance structures. As citizens become aware of the magnitude of corruption and the lack of accountability of their leaders, there will be growing social unrest and discontent that will challenge the very foundations of the established order.
Pluto in Aquarius will not only reveal the shames of the powerful, but will also question the validity of the models

of political representation and decision-making that have predominated until now. Representative democracy, so praised and defended, will be subjected to rigorous scrutiny, as its tendency to become corrupt and move away from the real interests of citizens will be revealed.

Likewise, Pluto's entry into this air sign will bring to light the limitations and biases inherent in information and communication systems controlled by elites. The manipulation of public opinion, the spread of fake news and the concentration of media power will be unmasked, undermining the credibility of traditional information channels and opening the way to new forms of access and circulation of knowledge.

This dynamic of revelation and dismantling of power structures will have a destabilizing effect on the current social and political order. However, far from being a chaotic and destructive process, the entry of Pluto into Aquarius represents a unique opportunity to rethink and rebuild the foundations of our societies in a more fair, transparent and democratic way. Exposing the weaknesses of power systems is the first step towards a deep and necessary transformation.

Radical changes in the exercise of power at a global level

The entry of Pluto into Aquarius will bring about a radical reconfiguration of geopolitical balances and the way power is exercised on a global scale. This planetary transit will mark the end of traditional models of global governance, based on the division of borders, zones of influence and power blocks, to give way to new dynamics of interaction and cooperation between nations and peoples.

One of the main effects of Pluto in Aquarius will be the erosion of the foundations of the established geopolitical order. The great powers that until now have shared the "pie" of global power will see their spheres of influence blur and be challenged by emerging factors that will drastically alter the international strategic landscape.

These new elements that will gain prominence under the influence of Pluto in Aquarius will be, to a large extent, technological in nature. Artificial intelligence, quantum computing, cyberwarfare and information manipulation will become crucially important in redefining power relations on a global scale.

Unlike traditional geopolitical models, based on the accumulation of physical resources and control of territories, these new technological factors will introduce a much more fluid and decentralized dynamic in the exercise of power. Physical borders will lose relevance, while the ability to dominate and exploit cyberspace, data and information flows will become the new currency in the global arena.

This transition towards a more "Aquarian" geopolitics will also imply a radical change in the way in which international conflicts are conceived and resolved. Pluto in Aquarius will give way to an era of "future vision wars", where different powers and blocs will confront each other not so much for the control of territories, but for the imposition of their respective visions and development models at a global level.

These "wars of the future" will be fought in the field of cyberwar, disinformation and the manipulation of public opinion, rather than on traditional battlefields. The ability to generate and disseminate alternative narratives, to influence electoral processes and to control data flows will become the new frontier of geopolitical dispute.

Likewise, Pluto in Aquarius will bring with it greater interdependence and cooperation between nations and regional blocs, to the detriment of the models of confrontation and competition that have predominated until now. The need to face global challenges, such as climate change, cybersecurity or the regulation of new technologies, will force States to rethink their strategies and seek more collaborative and multilateral solutions.

In this context, the emergence of new actors, such as citizen groups, non-governmental organizations and virtual communities, will have a significant impact on the reconfiguration of power at a global level. These agents, empowered by technology and the Aquarian vision of the future, will challenge the monopoly of States and large corporations in making decisions that affect humanity as a whole.

In summary, the entry of Pluto into Aquarius will mark the beginning of an era of profound changes in world geopolitics. The erosion of traditional power models, the emergence of new technological factors and the greater interdependence between nations and non-state actors will lead to a radical reconfiguration of the global strategic landscape.

New forms of organization and collective action

The entry of Pluto into Aquarius will not only reveal the weaknesses and abuses of established power systems, but will also give way to the emergence of new forms of organization and collective action. This sign, associated with vision of the future, technology and community spirit, will become the stage where transformative alternatives to current governance and citizen participation models are forged.

One of the key aspects of this Plutonian transit will be the empowerment of groups and social networks as agents of change. Aquarius, with its emphasis on cooperation, innovation and the search for common solutions, will foster the emergence of movements and organizations that will challenge the *status quo* from a more horizontal and participatory perspective.

Unlike the hierarchical and vertical models that have predominated until now, these new groups will be characterized by a more decentralized and democratic structure, where decision-making is carried out in a more inclusive and consensual manner. The Aquarian vision of the future, based on global interconnection and collaboration between peoples and nations, will become the common thread that will unite these groups around shared objectives and aspirations.

Under the influence of Pluto, these groups will acquire unprecedented strength and determination to promote radical transformations in various areas. From the political and economic to the social and cultural spheres, these movements will emerge as agents of change, questioning and dismantling old models of representation and citizen participation.

Technology, particularly communication and network organization tools, will play a fundamental role in strengthening these Aquarian groups. The ability to connect people from different latitudes, to share information and to coordinate actions in an agile and decentralized manner, will give them a strategic advantage in their fight to reconfigure the political and social landscape.

Likewise, the entry of Pluto into Aquarius will lead to the emergence of new social classes and economic models that will challenge the dominance of traditional capitalism.

These "cyber communities" or "technoelites" will be characterized by a more holistic and sustainable vision of development, prioritizing collaboration, innovation and collective well-being over the mere accumulation of wealth and power.

In this context, we will witness the creation of new social contracts, where the relationships between rulers and governed are redefined around principles of greater transparency, accountability and citizen participation. These agreements, the result of collective action and a shared vision of the future, will lay the foundations for the construction of more just, equitable and resilient societies.

The entry of Pluto into Aquarius, therefore, will not only reveal the weaknesses of existing power systems, but will also open the door to the emergence of new forms of organization and collective action, capable of driving deep and lasting transformations in our lives. societies.

The role of groups and common visions of the future

Under the influence of Pluto, these Aquarian groups will acquire unprecedented strength and determination to promote radical changes in various areas. They will no longer be mere interest or pressure groups, but true engines of social, political and cultural transformation.

What will unite these groups will not be so much a feeling of emotional belonging, as is often the case with more traditional groups, but rather a shared vision of the future. Aquarius, with its emphasis on innovation and the search for innovative solutions, will become the common thread that will unite these movements around common objectives and aspirations.

Far from being homogeneous and monolithic groups, these Aquarian groups will be characterized by their diversity and their ability to integrate different perspectives. Tolerance and open-mindedness will be fundamental features of these organizations, which will seek to build consensus from the richness of plurality.

Technology will give them a strategic advantage in their struggle to reconfigure the political and social landscape.

Beyond specific demands or sectoral interests, these Aquarian groups will emerge as true agents of change, questioning and dismantling old models of representation and citizen participation. Its objective will be the construction of a shared vision of the future, which transcends traditional borders and divisions.

In this sense, the groups that emerge under the influence of Pluto in Aquarius will distance themselves from the more emotional or identity-based movements, to embrace a more rational, strategic perspective oriented towards the solution of global problems. Its focus will be on the creation of new paradigms and models of social organization, more in line with the needs and aspirations of humanity in the coming era.

The ability of these groups to articulate and disseminate alternative visions of the future will be fundamental in the reconfiguration of the political and social landscape. Faced with traditional models of representation, based on division and confrontation, these movements will propose more collaborative and participatory forms of decision-making, which actively involve citizens.

In short, the role of groups and common visions of the future will be crucial in the era of Pluto in Aquarius. These agents of change, empowered by technology and the search for innovative solutions, will emerge as the main drivers of the transformations that will shake our societies in the coming decades.

The emergence of new social classes and social contracts

Parallel to the proliferation of groups and social movements empowered by the entry of Pluto into Aquarius, we will also witness the emergence of new social classes and economic models that will challenge the dominance of traditional capitalism.

These "cyber communities" or "technoelites" will be characterized by a more holistic and sustainable vision of development, prioritizing collaboration, innovation and collective well-being over the mere accumulation of wealth and power.

Unlike traditional elites, anchored in structures of privilege and exploitation, these new emerging classes will seek to establish a more harmonious and reciprocal relationship with society as a whole. Their objective will not be simply to maintain and increase their position of dominance, but rather to become inspiring agents and facilitators of social transformation.

Technology, and in particular innovations in areas such as artificial intelligence, quantum computing and genetics, will play a key role in shaping these new social classes. Far from being mere consumers or passive users of these advances, these groups will seek to dominate and exploit the possibilities offered by new technologies to drive large-scale transformations.

Likewise, the emergence of these Aquarian "techno-elites" will be accompanied by the creation of new social contracts, which will redefine the relationships between rulers and the governed. These agreements, the result of collective action and a shared vision of the future, will lay the foundations for the construction of more just, equitable and resilient societies.

Unlike traditional social contracts, based on division and confrontation between classes, these new pacts will seek to establish a strategic alliance between the emerging elites and the general public. The objective will be to align the interests of both sectors around common objectives of sustainable development, well-being and collective progress.

These Aquarian social contracts will be characterized by greater transparency in decision-making, more effective accountability of leaders, and more active participation of citizens in public affairs. Far from being imposed unilaterally, they will be the result of a process of negotiation and consensus between the different parties involved.

The emergence of these new social classes and social contracts represents a fundamental challenge to the models of power and governance that have predominated until now. Under the influence of Pluto in Aquarius, we will witness a radical reconfiguration of the socioeconomic landscape, where the old elites will be forced to adapt or give up their dominant position in favor of more equitable and participatory structures.

Revolutions in the era of Pluto in Aquarius

The entry of Pluto into Aquarius will not only bring with it a radical reconfiguration of geopolitical balances and the way in which power is exercised on a global scale, but will also trigger a series of profound revolutions in various areas of our society.

Technological and scientific revolution

One of the main drivers of transformation in the era of Pluto in Aquarius will be the technological and scientific revolution. This planetary transit will coincide with significant advances in fields such as artificial intelligence, quantum computing and genetics, which will have a disruptive impact on multiple spheres of life.

Pluto, with its affinity for the mysteries of life and transformation processes, will become a catalyst for these scientific and technological developments. Cybernetics, biotechnology and exploring the limits of the human genome will be some of the areas that will gain crucial importance in this new era.

These innovations will not only affect the productive and economic sectors, but will also have profound implications for the way we relate, organize ourselves and conceive our own identity. The integration of technology in the body and the possibility of diversifying the human species will be topics that will gain relevance in the coming decades.

Economic and financial revolution

In parallel with the technological revolution, the entry of Pluto into Aquarius will also lead to a radical transformation of the current economic and financial systems. We will witness a transition from the highly centralized and extractive models of the Earth era, towards more decentralized structures oriented to knowledge and human capital.

Large monolithic companies, such as Amazon, Google or Meta, will see their dominant positions challenged by new actors and business models more in line with the Aquarian vision. The emergence of "cyber communities" and "technoelites" that prioritize collaboration, innovation and collective well-being, rather than the mere accumulation of wealth, will be a characteristic feature of this economic revolution.

Likewise, we will witness the proliferation of new forms of exchange and transaction, such as cryptocurrencies and decentralized finance systems, which will challenge the monopoly of traditional financial systems. The regulation and control of these new economic instruments will be topics of great relevance in the coming decades.

Personal, psychological and social revolution

Beyond the transformations in the technological and economic spheres, the entry of Pluto into Aquarius will also trigger a revolution on the personal, psychological and social level.

In the field of psychology, Pluto in this air sign will lead us to deeply rethink our notions of identity, sexuality and interpersonal relationships. The deconstruction of gender archetypes and the reappropriation of astrological symbols traditionally associated with the masculine and feminine will be key processes in this transformation.

Likewise, Pluto in Aquarius will lead us towards a "mass psychology", where the psychic and emotional problems that we have dealt with individually will acquire a social and collective dimension. Understanding how our living and working conditions affect our mental health will be essential in this process.

In the social sphere, the entry of Pluto into this revolutionary sign will give rise to profound changes in power structures and in models of organization and citizen participation. The crisis of representative democracies and the emergence of more horizontal and participatory forms of decision-making will be some of the distinctive features of this social revolution.

In summary, the era of Pluto in Aquarius will be characterized by a succession of radical transformations on the technological, economic, psychological and social levels. These revolutions, although they may generate turbulence and unrest at first, also represent a unique opportunity to reconfigure our societies in accordance with the principles of the Aquarian vision: cooperation, innovation and the search for common solutions to the challenges of society. humanity.

Predictions and prospects

Beyond the profound transformations that the entry of Pluto into Aquarius will bring with it in the technological, economic, social and psychological fields, let us investigate a series of perspectives on some changes that could occur in the coming years.

The decline of large cities
and the rise of self-sufficient communities

Another prediction raised is the decline of large cities as we know them today. The city, as a tool of control and accumulation of power characteristic of the age of Earth, will lose its reason for being in the age of Aquarius.

Various factors, such as climate change and the search for more sustainable lifestyles, will lead people to move away from large cities and organize themselves into smaller, self-sufficient communities. These new forms of settlement, which could house hundreds to a few thousand inhabitants, will be characterized by greater autonomy in terms of resources, energy and food production.

The diversification of the human species and the integration of technology in the body

Another prediction raised is the possibility that, under the influence of Pluto in Aquarius, we will witness a diversification of the human species. This would imply the emergence of different "subspecies" or variants of humanity, a product of the increasingly deeper integration of technology into our bodies and organisms.

Although this scenario may seem like something out of science fiction, in reality we are already immersed in a process of hybridization between the biological and the artificial. From the use of glasses and hearing aids to the implantation of pacemakers and prostheses, humans have been incorporating technology into their bodies throughout history.

Under the influence of Pluto in Aquarius, this process of technological integration could accelerate and deepen, giving rise to forms of life beyond the traditional limits of the human species. This diversification raises ethical and existential questions that must be addressed in the coming decades.

The consolidation of teleworking

Another possibility is the consolidation of teleworking, a phenomenon that accelerated during the COVID-19 pandemic and could be strengthened in the coming years.

The entry of Pluto into Aquarius, together with the influence of Uranus in Gemini, will favor the proliferation of remote work modalities. This is because the hierarchical control and supervision models, characteristic of the Earth era, will come into tension with the more horizontal and decentralized vision of Aquarius.

Likewise, a large number of tasks and functions that are currently carried out in person could be carried out remotely, with significant savings in terms of time, energy and pollution. This scenario poses challenges in terms of redefining labor relations and work organization.

Possible limits on maximum salaries

Finally, another possibility, in the context of the era of Pluto in Aquarius, is that limits are established on the maximum salaries that top executives and economic elites can receive.

The growing inequality and the perception of social injustice that characterizes the current capitalist system could lead to the implementation of measures that put a stop to the enormous wage gaps. This would respond to a more equitable vision oriented toward collective well-being, typical of the Aquarian era.

The argument that high salaries are necessary to retain the "top talent" is unsupported, and that it is morally unacceptable that a person can earn thousands of times more than the minimum wage. Therefore, it suggests that the establishment of salary caps could be one of the transformations that occur in the coming decades.

APPENDIX I

Sign by Sign Forecast
of Pluto Transit in Aquarius.

The effects of a Pluto transit

Pluto moves in aspect to a person's Sun, Moon or Ascendant, their life will be transformed, especially if these planets are in Aquarius. A Pluto transit is a life-changing event, but there is nothing to be afraid of.

Life is constantly changing, like the body's cells dying and regenerating. Our emotions, our bodies and our circumstances are constantly changing. However, we often create a mental image that holds on to a particular way of being, whether in our appearance, relationships, or finances. When Pluto moves in a person's natal chart, it will show them that none of it was lasting, that nothing they thought they had was going to stay the same forever. Furthermore, the person has no control over what that change will look like. This change is not necessarily a bad thing. Even the most horrible events can become great blessings. It is not helpful to judge events as good or bad, as that is a superficial way of looking at life. The important thing is to understand how the person evolves along with the area of life that Pluto is transforming.

The Pluto transit is not something that is happening to the person, but something that they must actively participate in. It is advisable to release the victim energy and be graceful in the process of change and transformation, since life is a constant process of letting go and accumulating.

Sign by Sign Forecast of Transit Pluto in Aquarius

Valid for people who have the Sun, the Moon or the Ascendant in each of the signs in their Natal Chart.

Aries

For Aries, Pluto will be transiting the 11th house, which will change your friendships and social groups quite a bit. Between now and 20 years from now, the people you associate with will be completely different.

This is not something that happens only to Aries, but it is something really radical. In addition, Aries' goals and dreams will also completely change. Initially, Aries may feel very committed to certain ideals, groups or plans, but Pluto will show that that is not actually what they need or want. Pluto can also affect Aries' ability to earn money. Since Pluto left the 10th house, everything related to career, marriage and social status has been completely transformed. Now, Aries will take that experience to the 11th house and will be able to recognize how they want to make money and from what activities.

Aries may also begin to meet powerful, wealthy or influential people who will appear in their life in a very confrontational or very supportive way. This will make you question many things in your life. Overall, Pluto in the 11th house will radically transform Aries' friendships, groups, goals, and income. It will be a period of much growth and learning.

Taurus

For Taurus, Pluto will be transiting the 10th house, which will mean a massive change in their social status and career. The original desires and ambitions that Taurus had are likely to be completely transformed.

Pluto can completely change the context in which one functions, including relationships with authority figures. If Taurus is already on the right path, Pluto will strengthen it. But if not, it will force you to find what you really want to do.

It is important to note that with Pluto in the 10th house, there may be power struggles with authority figures. Taurus will have to learn to be their own authority without abusing power. You will need to ensure that you act with ethical integrity, as you will be very visible during this transit.

In general, Pluto will radically transform the career and social status of Taurus. This may involve changes in income and wealth, either towards more or less. The important thing is that Taurus learns to find their own inner power, instead of seeking power over others.

Gemini

For Gemini, Pluto will be transiting the 9th house, which is considered a quite favorable place for this transit.

Pluto in the 9th house can greatly expand Gemini's worldview, both on a material and esoteric level. It can lead Gemini to travel a lot, not for vacations, but to learn and grow. The speaker mentions that during this transit, she was able to absorb information in a way she had not been able to before.

Additionally, Pluto in the 9th house can change Gemini's relationship with his father or father figures, from either a more challenging way to a more balanced one.

Another positive aspect is that Gemini can develop a great interest in teaching or communicating ideas. You may feel an urge to share knowledge and life philosophies in a deeper and purposeful way.

Overall, Pluto in the 9th will provide Gemini with an opportunity to greatly expand their horizons, their spiritual understanding, and their way of communicating and teaching. It will be a period of growth and transformation, although the speaker warns against falling into dogmatism or proselytism.

Cancer

For Cancer, Pluto will be transiting the 8th house, which can be quite an intimidating transit for many. It is important to reevaluate that perception, as it can be an opportunity to confront unconscious processes. Pluto in the 8th house can bring losses. This will help Cancer reflect on the meaning of life and death, and how they are interconnected.

On a financial level, Cancer can transform your relationship with other people's money, such as inheritances or changes in the social and financial status of parents. This will require Cancer to take more control and responsibility over their own money.

The 8th house is also a place of deep spiritual transformation. Cancer may become more interested in the secrets of life and metaphysical aspects. This may lead to exploring occult or mystical practices, although caution is cautioned against negative influences.

Pluto in the 8th house can also bring health problems, both physical and mental. It is important for Cancer to seek help and support if they feel depression or lack of connection. This will require a framework, whether social or spiritual, to guide the process.

Leo

For Leo, Pluto will be transiting the 7th house, which is a time of powerful change in terms of your relationships. This means that Leo will also have to change along with those relationships. Leo's marriage or any long-term relationship will change. This can even affect business or customer relationships. Pluto will dismantle the way Leo sees himself in terms of relationships and partnerships. This is not necessarily destructive, but will allow you to align in a more harmonious way with who you really are at this moment. Pluto will show where Leo is giving up his power, allowing others to dominate him. By learning this lesson, Leo will understand that his own power is enough and he does not have to surrender to others. Leo is advised to take a critical look at his relationships and, if necessary, seek the help of a therapist for more clarity. Changes in relationships are inevitable, but this will bring you closer to yourself.

Overall, Leo will experience a dramatic transformation of himself, his home life, his social status, and the people he spends time with over the next 20 years. Although it may be challenging, it is necessary for your personal growth.

Virgo

For Virgo, Pluto will be transiting the 6th house, which is a fairly familiar place, as it is Virgo's natural house in the zodiac. This will completely transform Virgo's life when it comes to their health and daily routines. Virgo can turn your health around if you face health challenges, as Pluto will help you resolve them. In addition to health changes, Pluto will also transform Virgo's work and daily routines. Virgo may initially feel like they are being challenged or deeply confused, without feeling like they are in the right place in their daily life. This will require adjustments, whether in the physical, diet, lifestyle or work itself. However, Virgo will feel a sense of progress as they go through these changes in the 6th house. They may even experience dramatic health problems. If Virgo works in health-related fields, this transit can be especially beneficial.

You may feel an inner calling to become a healthcare provider or improve the health of others through your work. Overall, Pluto will radically transform Virgo's health and daily work. It will be a period of challenges, but also of growth and development of valuable skills.

Libra

For Libra, Pluto will be transiting the 5th house, which is a relatively soft place for this transit.

If Libra has children, this will transform the relationship with them, whether between parent and child or in the role of authority. Possible power struggles in this area.

Pluto can also change Libra's desire to have children. As a parent, Libra will have a huge influence on his children during this transit. This can be both positive and negative, so it is suggested to consider training in non-violent communication or *mindfulness* for parenting. If Libra doesn't have children or it's not time anymore, he can channel that creative energy into other projects that are like "babies" for him.

Pluto in the 5th house can also cause Libra to become more competitive in sports, turning them from amateur to professional. This can be a source of pleasure or even income.

However, we warn against becoming obsessed with games and betting, which can lead to large profits or losses.

Romance and love can also be affected, leading Libra to become intensely involved in a relationship.

Scorpio

For Scorpio, Pluto will be transiting the 4th house, which is a very intense place, but Scorpio is prepared for it.

Pluto in the 4th house will make Scorpio feel very agitated and will have to understand himself from a very deep place, going back to his childhood and his relationship with his mother.

The 4th house represents what makes us happy and makes us feel secure and stable in life. With Pluto here, Scorpio will feel very shaken, especially at first, and will have to understand where that feeling of security comes from.

Initially, Scorpio may look to the outside world, in objects and money, for that feeling of security. But eventually you will realize that true stability comes from within you, from your ability to constantly transform and transmute.

Pluto in the 4th house can also affect investments, property, and housing matters. It may lead Scorpio to buy a house or get rid of one, depending on how he feels about security.

Possible obsessive tendencies with property or security, which may actually be more destabilizing than stabilizing.

Pluto can also polarize Scorpio's emotional relationships, especially with family. There may be drastic changes in the way Scorpio relates to loved ones.

Scorpio is advised to seek help, whether through therapy or practices such as family constellations, to process these changes constructively.

Overall, Pluto in the 4th house will be a very transformative transit for Scorpio, allowing you to understand yourself and your family relationships on a deep level. It will be a challenging period, but also one of growth.

Sagitarius

For Sagittarius, Pluto will be transiting the 3rd house, which is a quite powerful and very interesting place to develop skills and will.

Pluto will give Sagittarius courage, but he will often have to find that courage through adversity, causing him to have to step up and find different ways to show himself.

This can affect your relationship with siblings, which can change dramatically, or your relationship with people in the neighborhood, where you will have to learn to stand up for yourself and balance those relationships.

Communication and the way Sagittarius expresses their voice will also be affected. There may be times when you realize that you are not speaking enough and others when you are too domineering and dogmatic in your way of communicating. You will have to learn to adapt.

Pluto can also make Sagittarius shy about communicating and will challenge you to step out of your comfort zone to express yourself, whether in the media or when starting a business.

All of this will greatly develop Sagittarius' sense of resilience and willpower. It will be a very dynamic time, although this will depend on other astrological factors.

The 3rd house also represents the hobbies and skills of Sagittarius. Pluto can cause you to refine and completely change the way you express your creativity, whether in art, writing, or music.

It is suggested that Sagittarius explore non-violent communication, as Pluto can take you to extremes, being too aggressive or too shy.

Additionally, Pluto in the 3rd house can be disruptive to mental health, causing problems such as depression or anxiety. Sagittarius should take care of their mental health and seek support from a community that supports them during this transit.

Overall, it will be a period of much personal growth for Sagittarius, where you will develop valuable skills and willpower through adversity.

Capricorn

For Capricorn, Pluto will be transiting the 2nd house, which is the house of money, income and everything that sustains you in life. This will entail a big change financially and in terms of your values.

Capricorn may experience a change in their perception of money and material possessions. You may feel like you don't care as much anymore or don't want to put in as much effort as you used to.

If Capricorn is someone who invests money, their investments, the value of their properties or their income can fluctuate quite a bit. There may be an initial shock that seems threatening, but over time it will stabilize.

These changes may come from a transformation in Capricorn's values, not just in the things around him, but in how he values himself and what he considers important in his life.

Pluto in the 2nd house is often an indicator of a very wealthy person. So financial changes can go in both directions, from having less to having much more.

Capricorn can go from feeling indifferent to money to developing a great disinterest or rejection of it. This can come from an awakening or a deeper understanding of what is truly valuable, beyond the material.

These changes in values can be both material and psychological. Since it is a very long transit, some of these transformations may be more hidden at the beginning.

Even consumption habits, whether food, drugs or alcohol, can be affected and transformed during this period. Capricorn will have to be careful not to fall into obsessions or addictions.

In general, Capricorn's way of life and material standards will change dramatically, either due to external circumstances or due to an internal transformation of their values and priorities.

Aquarius

For Aquarius, Pluto will be transiting the 1st house for 20 years, whether it is your ascendant, your sun or your moon. This will be a radical transformation, whether for better or worse.

The type of change Aquarius will experience will depend on how you manage your own life and physical body, as the 1st house represents the self and self.

Aquarius may experience physical changes in their appearance throughout these 20 years. You may have health problems or decide to change your weight, exercise, etc. But Pluto will also show you where there is too much ego involved in your life.

Since Aquarius sometimes has a strong ego, Pluto will be tasked with dismantling that so you can get closer to your true self. This can lead to power struggles with people in the 7th house, opposite Aquarius.

Pluto in the 1st house will affect the fundamental pillars of the Aquarius map, such as the 4th house (emotions and home), the 7th house (relationships) and the 10th house (career). This will challenge and change many areas of your life.

Aquarius may decide for the first time in his life to put his foot down and take on a role he didn't dare to do before. Or realizing that you've been taking up too much space and need to be more humble.

Aquarius must be attentive to his ego and his desires, since a lack of humility is a shadow of Aquarius. Pluto in the 1st house will help you understand aspects of yourself that have been limiting you.
This transit will be a challenge, but a powerful ally for the spiritual growth of Aquarius, if you are on a path of self-knowledge. Your personality can change dramatically, from shy to powerful and leader.

However, Aquarius must be careful not to overwhelm others or create enemies, as Pluto in the 1st house can lead to conflict and manipulation. It will be important to get feedback from others on how they see you.

In general, Aquarius will face 20 years of profound changes, where he will have to let go of a false image of himself and discover his true self. It will be a challenging period, but also one of great growth and expansion.

Pisces

For Pisces, Pluto will be transiting the 12th house, which is a fairly familiar place energetically, as Pisces is the natural sign of the 12th house.

The 12th house is about endings and possible losses, so Pisces will be "shedding his skin" and really understanding the true nature of life and his purpose in it.

Depending on the age of Pisces, this transit may be a step before Pluto enters your 1st house, which will entail a personal transformation and revelation. But if Pisces is older, this may be the time to let go of everything you believe you are and everything you have accumulated, both materially and psychologically.

Pluto will have a powerful effect on the Pisces unconscious, bringing old patterns and unresolved issues to the surface. This can make Pisces feel emotionally immature or unable to deal with things.

If Pisces finds himself escaping through alcohol, drugs, or avoiding life, even through spiritual practices, this may be a form of avoidance that isn't really helping him.

Instead, Pluto in the 12th house is an invitation for Pisces to understand the depths of their mind and free themselves from what is dragging them down in this life. It may be a time to eliminate things, simplify and lighten the load.

If Pisces has problems with addictions or self-destructive behaviors, Pluto will make them aware of the harmful effects they are causing themselves. This can be difficult, but also one of the best things that can happen to you to overcome those problems.

Pluto in the 12th house can also awaken in Pisces the desire to travel or retreat to remote places or spiritual retreat.

Overall, this transit will invite Pisces to deeply understand the continuity of life beyond the physical, and to be honest with themselves about what needs to change. It will be a period of much internal transformation.

APPENDIX II

Meanings of Pluto in
the 12 Astrological Houses.

Pluto as a point of the past and its importance in personal evolution

Pluto is considered one of the most important past points in astrology, along with the Moon and the South Node. This is because Pluto represents those patterns of behavior, beliefs and attachments that have become a kind of "comfort zone" for our ego.

The birth chart, in this sense, can be used as a map of the evolutionary process of our soul through incarnations. It shows us where we come from, the conditioning and experiences we have lived in the past, and where we are going in this particular life. What astrology calls "past points" are those areas of our lives in which we tend to repeat patterns, feel more secure and exercise greater control.

Pluto, as the largest of these points in the past, tells us which area of our life is the one that obsesses us the most, that generates the most anguish and a feeling of lack of control when things don't go the way we want. It's that part of us that desperately clings to maintaining control, to getting what we want, even if to do so we must resort to manipulation, lying, or a lack of empathy.

This Plutonian energy arises because, deep down, we have a deep fear of losing control, of unleashing what we fear so much will happen. It's as if we have a "dragon" breathing down our neck, ready to destroy us if we fail to maintain control of our lives. And it is precisely in the astrological house where Pluto is located in our natal map that this pattern manifests itself.

However, the evolution that life proposes to us is not what we normally believe. It's not about getting what we want, about being happy and successful. Evolution implies that our controlling and selfish ego loses strength, giving way to a greater connection with our essence, with our deepest being. It is an uncomfortable process for the ego, but necessary for our personality to become more consistent with who we really are.

Pluto, in this sense, becomes a fundamental guide towards this evolution. It shows us what we are most attached to, what most obsesses and controls us, so that we can release those patterns and open ourselves to a way of living more aligned with our soul. It is not a simple process, as it involves facing our greatest fears and giving up what gives us a false sense of security. But it is precisely in that delivery, in that surrender, where true strength and power emerges, which does not depend on controlling the external world, but on connecting with our deepest essence.

The birth chart as a map of the evolutionary process

Astrology offers us a powerful tool to understand our personal evolution process: the birth chart. Far from being a simple prediction of the future, the birth chart can be used as a map showing us where we have come from and where we are going in our current incarnation.

The birth chart reveals two fundamental aspects to us: the past of our soul and the new learning that we have come to experience in this life. "Past points" are those areas of our lives in which we tend to repeat patterns, feel more secure, and exert more control. These past points are mainly represented by the Moon, the South Node and, above all, Pluto.

Pluto, as the largest of these points in the past, tells us which area of our life is the one that obsesses us the most, that generates the most anguish and a feeling of lack of control when things don't go the way we want. It's that part of us that desperately clings to maintaining control, to getting what we want, even if to do so we must resort to manipulation, lying, or a lack of empathy. But the birth chart also shows us what is new, what expands our level of consciousness and leads us to experience different learning. Many times, our personal drama lies precisely in the fact that we resist letting go of the old, the known, to embrace the new that life offers us.

Understanding this dynamic is key, since evolution is not what we normally believe. It's not about getting what we want, about being happy and successful. Evolution implies that our controlling and selfish ego loses strength, giving way to a greater connection with our essence, with our deepest being. It is an uncomfortable process for the ego, but necessary for our personality to become more consistent with who we really are.

In this sense, the birth chart becomes an invaluable map to guide us in this evolutionary process. It shows us those areas of our lives where we are most attached, where we are most obsessed and controlled, so that we can release those patterns and open ourselves to a way of living more aligned with our soul.

Understanding the information that the birth chart provides us, especially with regard to the location of Pluto, then becomes essential to embark on this journey of personal transformation. It allows us to identify our greatest points of resistance, our deepest fears, and thus be able to face them with courage and dedication. Only in this way can we free ourselves from what ties us to the past, to embrace the new that life offers us in every moment.

Pluto in House I

Attachment to individuality and control

When Pluto is located in House I of the natal chart, we are faced with one of the most powerful and challenging positionings on this planet. House I, also known as the House of Self, represents our individuality, our way of expressing ourselves and projecting ourselves in the world.

Individuals with Pluto in House I usually have a huge attachment and obsession with controlling and dominating everything around them. There is a constant feeling that they must maintain control over their own life and their own identity, otherwise they feel that they can be destroyed or violated.

This Plutonian energy manifests itself even from childhood. When working with babies who have Pluto in House I, it is observed that they tend to cry constantly, to always be angry and suffering. This is because, in its helpless condition, the baby does not have any type of power or control, which generates tremendous anguish and a feeling of vulnerability.

As these individuals grow, this need for control and to feel powerful becomes even more accentuated. They can develop a very individualistic and selfish personality, where the only thing that matters is satisfying their own desires, regardless of the impact they may have on others. They are willing to do anything to take life in the direction they want.

In addition, people with Pluto in the 1st House usually have experienced traumatic and violent experiences during childbirth or in their early childhood. This generates a constant fear of being attacked, destroyed or violated, which leads them to adopt a defensive attitude and hide their true essence.

However, the challenge posed by Pluto in House I is to learn to let go of that control, to allow life to transform them and to put its power at the service of the human collective. They must understand that their true strength lies not in dominating and manipulating, but in connecting with their deepest essence and allowing it to guide their path.
It is a process of deep introspection and surrender, as it involves facing those primordial fears and learning to trust in life, despite the traumatic experiences experienced. Only in this way will they be able to

unleash their true potential and become agents of change and transformation in the world.

Face the fear of being destroyed

One of the deepest challenges that people with Pluto in the 1st House face is the constant fear of being destroyed or violated. This feeling of vulnerability and helplessness originates from traumatic experiences experienced during childbirth or in early childhood.

When Pluto, the planet of transformation and symbolic death, is located in House I, which represents one's own identity and sense of self, a very intense dynamic is generated. There is an enormous attachment and obsession to maintain control and power over one's own life, otherwise a deep terror of being annihilated arises.

These people often feel that they must constantly protect themselves, that they must hide their true essence to avoid being attacked or violated. There is an inherent distrust of the world and others, fearing that if they show themselves as they are, they will be destroyed.

In some cases, these people may seek relationships with controlling and dominant people, because they feel that this way they will be able to maintain a certain sense of security. However, this only perpetuates the cycle of fear and disempowerment.

The challenge lies in these people being able to face that primordial fear, that terror of being annihilated. They must find the courage to go out into the world and live according to their true essence, allowing life to transform them, instead of trying to obsessively control it.

This involves a process of deep introspection and surrender. They must learn to trust life, to let go of control and to allow changes and transformations to occur, no matter how painful they may be. Only in this way will they be able to unleash their true power, which lies not in domination and manipulation, but in the connection with their deepest essence.

It is a challenging path, as it requires facing those ancestral fears that have been engraved in the soul. But it is precisely in that dedication and surrender where a truly transformative strength and potential emerges, which will allow them to become agents of change and evolution, both on a personal and collective level.

Pluto in House II

Attachment to stability and resistance to change

When Pluto, the planet of transformation and symbolic death, is located in House II of the birth chart, we find ourselves facing a strong attachment to stability and a deep resistance to change.

House II represents a person's values, resources and material security. When Pluto is positioned here, there is an overwhelming fear of losing that sense of stability and control over one's assets and finances.

These people usually have a motto that says "rather dead than change." There is an enormous inertia that prevents them from embracing the transformations and new experiences that life presents them. There is a deep attachment to keeping things as they are, without allowing anything to move or be altered.

This fear of change also extends to one's introspection and looking inward. There is a great fear of facing one's own shadow, one's own darkness, because that could trigger a crisis that puts at risk that feeling of security that one so longs for.

There are two types of people with Pluto in House II: those who work tirelessly to accumulate money and goods, believing that this will give them the stability they need, and those who completely reject money and material resources, as a form of resistance. to that attachment.

In both cases, the challenge lies in releasing that obsessive control over stability and learning to embrace transformations. You must understand that true abundance lies not in accumulating possessions, but in allowing changes to occur and trusting that you will be able to adapt to them.

This involves a process of introspection and connection with one's own emotions and fears. Only by facing that feeling of insecurity and vulnerability will you be able to release your true potential for abundance and prosperity, without needing to cling to material things.

The path of evolution with Pluto in House II is to learn to let go of control, to embrace uncertainty and to trust that life will guide you towards the stability and security that you so long for, but from a deeper and more authentic place, which do not depend exclusively on the material.

Relationship with abundance and money

When Pluto is located in House II of the birth chart, the person's relationship with abundance and money is usually a central theme in their evolution process.

There are two types of people who can present this positioning of Pluto. On the one hand, there are those who work tirelessly to accumulate money and assets, believing that this will provide them with the stability and security they so desperately need. These people are usually obsessed with having control over their resources, even going so far as to manipulate and dishonestly in order to obtain them.
On the other hand, there are those who completely reject money and material resources, as a form of resistance to that attachment that generates so much fear in them. These people may have deep-rooted family beliefs or programming that prevent them from recognizing and accepting their own desire for abundance.

In both cases, the challenge lies in releasing that obsessive control over money and learning to trust that life will guide you towards the stability and prosperity you need, but from a deeper and more authentic place.

When someone with Pluto in the Second House has financial problems, this is usually because they are holding on to something, a belief, or a pattern that is preventing them from opening up to their highest level of abundance. There is a fear of letting go of what you have, for fear of losing that feeling of security.

However, Pluto in House II can also generate a lot of abundance, especially when the person manages to release that obsessive control and allow changes and transformations to occur in their relationship with money and resources.

The challenge is to learn to look at your own emotions and beliefs around money, face those fears of insecurity and instability, and allow life to guide you toward a more fluid and confident way of relating to abundance.

This implies a process of introspection and connection with one's own essence, beyond family or social programming and conditioning. Only in this way will they be able to unleash their true potential for prosperity, without needing to cling to material things as the only source of security.

Pluto in House III
The obsession with understanding and having all the answers

When Pluto is located in House III of the birth chart, the person's mind is usually dominated by an obsession with understanding and having all the possible answers.

House III represents the mind, communication and intellect. When Pluto, the planet of transformation and symbolic death, is positioned here, there is an urgent need to understand and explain everything that happens around you.

These people are usually very curious and very intellectual. They are constantly thinking, analyzing, searching for information and trying to find the answers to all their concerns.

However, this desire to understand everything can become a true obsession that prevents them from really listening and processing the information they receive. There is a constant anxiety to have all the explanations, which prevents them from being silent and allowing integration and deep understanding to occur naturally.

There is a very graphic metaphor to illustrate this pattern: it is as if the person were constantly eating, without giving their stomach time to properly process the food. In the same way, the minds of these people never stop, which prevents them from reaching true wisdom.

One of the challenges that Pluto in House III poses is learning to be silent, to look at the "dragon" of thoughts without needing to have all the answers. They must allow themselves the emptiness, the not knowing, so that their unconscious can process the information and lead them to a deeper understanding.

In addition, Pluto in House III can also generate destructive thoughts and violent use of words. These people must learn to take care of their communication, not to use their intellect as a tool of manipulation or attack.

The path of evolution with Pluto in House III involves developing the ability to meditate, to be silent and to allow information to be integrated naturally, without the obsessive need to understand everything. Only in this way will they be able to unleash their true intellectual and communicative potential, in the service of a deeper and more transformative understanding.

Learn to be silent and process information

One of the key challenges that Pluto poses in House III of the birth chart is the need to learn to be silent and properly process the information that is received.

People with this Pluto positioning are often obsessed with understanding and having all the possible answers. There is a mind constantly active, analyzing, seeking information and trying to find explanations for everything that happens around it.

However, this desire to understand and explain everything can become a real trap. In the same way, the minds of these people never stop, which prevents them from reaching true wisdom.

The challenge lies in learning to be silent, to allow yourself to be empty and not knowing. Only in this way will they be able to give space for the information they receive to be integrated naturally, without the obsessive need to understand everything immediately.

When someone with Pluto in House III manages to be silent and walk in peace, that is when their unconscious can process that information and lead them to a deeper understanding. It is in that space of stillness and receptivity where true wisdom arises.

This involves a process of learning and personal transformation. These people must develop the ability to meditate, to be in touch with their inner world, without the constant need to have all the answers. They must learn to trust that the information will integrate naturally, without forcing understanding. In addition, Pluto in House III can also generate destructive thoughts and violent use of words. Therefore, another key aspect of this evolutionary process is learning to take care of communication, not to use intellect as a tool of manipulation or attack.

In summary, the path with Pluto in House III involves developing the ability to be silent, to allow emptiness and to trust that information will be processed naturally. Only in this way will they be able to unleash their true intellectual and communicative potential, in the service of a deeper and more transformative understanding.

Pluto in House IV

Traumatic experiences in the home and family

When Pluto, the planet of transformation and symbolic death, is located in House IV of the birth chart, it is very likely that the person has experienced traumatic experiences in their home and family environment during their childhood.

The IV House represents the home, family, origins and emotional roots of an individual. When Pluto is positioned here, this indicates that in the environment where the person grew up, there was a very intense energy, loaded with drama, pain, manipulation and control.

One parent, or even both, may have been very controlling, domineering, or even violent. The home became a space of transformation and symbolic death, where the person had to face situations of great emotional intensity.

These traumatic experiences experienced in childhood, whether due to abortions, losses or family conflicts, were recorded in the person's cellular memory. Although you cannot consciously remember them, that emotional charge is still present and manifests itself in your adult life.

In some cases, these people may have developed a deep fear of the intensity of their own emotions. They are terrified of losing control and of their feelings overflowing, because they fear that this could lead to destruction.

This pattern is reflected in the way these people relate to their home and family in adulthood. They can become obsessive about maintaining control and emotional security, even manipulating or destroying those closest to them, in order to preserve that feeling of protection.

The challenge posed by Pluto in House IV is learning to look at and process those intense emotions that originated in childhood. They must face the fear of abandonment and disintegration, in order to develop a greater capacity for self-regulation and connection with their inner world.

Only by healing these ancestral wounds can you find true emotional security, not through control and manipulation, but through acceptance and trust in life.

This is a deep transformation process that will allow you to unleash your potential and establish healthier and more harmonious bonds.

Attachment to emotional security

When Pluto is located in House IV of the birth chart, one of the person's main attachments focuses on the search for emotional security, for a "nest" where they can feel protected and calm.

The IV House represents the home, family and emotional roots of an individual. Since Pluto, the planet of transformation and symbolic death, is positioned here, this indicates that the person has lived through traumatic and intense experiences in their family environment during childhood.

The home of these people may have been a space full of drama, manipulation and control, where one or both parents were very dominant and violent. These experiences were recorded in the person's cellular memory, generating a deep fear of losing that feeling of security and protection.

In their adult lives, the main attachment of these people focuses on maintaining that emotional stability at all costs. They are willing to do whatever is necessary, even manipulate or destroy those closest to them, in order to preserve that sense of calm and control in their home.

These people usually have a very intense "inner child" that overwhelms them emotionally and that they don't know how to calm down. There is a great fear of losing control of their own emotions, as they fear that this could lead to destruction.

The challenge posed by Pluto in House IV is learning to process and integrate those intense emotions that originated in childhood. They must face the fear of abandonment and disintegration, in order to develop a greater capacity for self-regulation and connection with their inner world.

Only by healing these ancestral wounds can you find true emotional security, not through control and manipulation, but through acceptance and trust in life. This is a deep transformation process that will allow you to unleash your potential and establish healthier and more harmonious bonds.

Pluto in House V

The attachment to applause
and the desire to be special

When Pluto is located in the V House of the birth chart, the person's main attachment focuses on the desire to be special, to stand out and to receive the applause and attention of others.

There are two different ways in which this positioning of Pluto can manifest. On the one hand, there are those people who have lived experiences of rejection and shame in the past, where they felt that they wanted to be more special than others, but they were not seen or recognized. This generates a rather shy and withdrawn personality, which builds a character or mask to adapt to what they believe others want to see, but deep down there is resentment for not being able to show themselves as they are.

On the other hand, there is a second group of people with Pluto in House V who are the complete opposite: they are very extroverted, creative and go on stage without fear of being seen. However, attachment in this case is also focused on what they do creatively being applauded and recognized by others. There is a need to be admired and to gain applause, rather than to express oneself authentically.

In both cases, the challenge lies in working on envy and the feeling of not being seen or valued. They must learn to allow themselves the process of transformation, to create for the simple pleasure of doing so, without paying attention to the public's reaction. Only in this way will they be able to release their true creative and expressive potential, without it being tied to the need to receive the applause and approval of others.

Another key aspect is learning to laugh at the ego and the importance they give to being special. This will allow them to let go of that obsession and connect more authentically with their creative essence, without having to adapt to other people's expectations.

In summary, the attachment to applause and the desire to be special is one of the main challenges posed by Pluto in House V. Overcoming it involves a process of introspection, acceptance of one's own worth beyond external recognition, and connection with creative expression for its own sake, without ties.

Two types of people with Pluto in House V

When Pluto is located in House V of the natal chart, there are two types of people who can present this positioning very differently.

On the one hand, there are those people who have experienced rejection and shame in the past. They felt a strong desire to be more special than others, to stand out and receive applause, but in reality they were not seen or recognized. This generates a rather shy and withdrawn personality, which builds a character or mask to adapt to what they believe others want to see.

Deep down, these people have resentment for not being able to show themselves as they are. They are afraid to go on stage and expose themselves, but at the same time they desperately crave applause and attention. It is a complex dynamic, where the only thing they really want is to be applauded.

On the other hand, there is a second group of people with Pluto in House V who are the complete opposite. They are very outgoing, creative and go on stage without fear of being seen. However, attachment in this case is also focused on what they do creatively being applauded and recognized by others. There is a need to be admired and to obtain applause, rather than to express oneself authentically.

In both cases, the challenge lies in working on envy and the feeling of not being seen or valued. They must learn to allow themselves the process of transformation, to create for the simple pleasure of doing so, without paying attention to the public's reaction. Only in this way will they be able to release their true creative and expressive potential, without it being tied to the need to receive the applause and approval of others.

Another key aspect is learning to laugh at the ego and the importance they give to being special. This will allow them to let go of that obsession and connect more authentically with their creative essence, without having to adapt to other people's expectations.

In summary, there are two types of people with Pluto in House V, with very different dynamics, but who share the challenge of letting go of the attachment to applause and external recognition, to be able to express themselves in a more genuine and liberating way.

Pluto in House VI

The obsession with perfection and service

When Pluto is located in House VI of the birth chart, the person usually develops a strong obsession with perfection and service to others.

These people are described as "super Virgo", in the sense that they work tirelessly, without stopping. They have a tendency to be very self-demanding, with enormous self-criticism towards their own imperfections. It is very difficult for them to set limits and say no, because they feel great guilt for not being able to meet all the demands.

There is a compulsion in them to serve and help others, but this becomes problematic when it becomes a way of avoiding looking at themselves. They have difficulty connecting with silence, rest and introspection, because they fear that doing so will bring up emotions and aspects of themselves that are uncomfortable for them.

The minds of these people are constantly focused on detecting flaws and problems, even in those areas where they have great gifts and talents. There is a tendency toward self-criticism and guilt, which can lead them to get sick, since their body ends up reflecting that lack of acceptance and self-pity.

The challenge posed by Pluto in House VI is to learn to accept imperfection, to allow chaos and disorder to be part of life without generating a crisis. They must release the need for control and demand, to be able to transform their vocation and direct it towards the service of the group, from a more authentic and balanced place.

This involves a process of introspection and connection with one's own repressed emotions. Only by healing this tendency to demand themselves will they be able to develop a greater capacity for self-care, for setting healthy limits, and for embracing imperfection as an inherent part of existence.

In summary, the obsession with perfection and service is one of the main challenges posed by Pluto in the VI House. Overcoming it requires a journey of acceptance, self-compassion and integration of the darker aspects of the self, in order to express the gifts in a more balanced and liberating way.

Learn to accept imperfection and chaos

One of the main challenges that Pluto poses in House VI of the birth chart is the need to learn to accept imperfection and chaos as an inherent part of existence.

These people are often described as "super Virgo", in the sense that they have an obsessive tendency to work tirelessly, without stopping. There is a compulsion in them to serve and help others, but this becomes problematic when it becomes a way of avoiding looking at themselves.

It is very difficult for them to set limits and say no, because they feel great guilt for not being able to meet all the demands. There is enormous self-criticism towards their own imperfections, which prevents them from connecting with silence, rest and introspection, because they fear that by doing so, emotions and aspects of themselves that are uncomfortable will arise.

The minds of these people are constantly focused on detecting flaws and problems, even in those areas where they have great gifts and talents. There is a tendency toward guilt and the feeling that something is wrong, which can lead them to get sick, since their body ends up reflecting that lack of acceptance and self-pity.

The challenge lies in these people being able to release the need for control and perfect demand. They must learn to accept imperfection, to allow chaos and disorder to be part of life without generating an internal crisis.

This involves a process of introspection and connection with one's own repressed emotions. Only by healing this tendency to demand themselves will they be able to develop a greater capacity for self-care, for setting healthy limits, and for embracing imperfection as an inherent part of existence.

By doing so, they will be able to transform their vocation and direct it towards the service of the group, from a more authentic and balanced place, without the need to sacrifice or deny their own needs.

Pluto in House VII

Attachment to relationships and intense bonds

When Pluto is located in House VII of the birth chart, the person's main attachment focuses on relationships and interpersonal ties.

As explained, these people have a compulsion to be with others, to have friends and partners. They can't stand the idea of being alone, feeling that their security and sense of identity depend on connection with others.

There is an intensity and total dedication in the bonds they establish, where the relationship becomes a matter of "life or death." They can develop very strong patterns of drama and emotional dependency, both in their family and relationship relationships.

Some of these people become possessive and controlling with their partners, seeking to maintain control and security at all costs. Others, on the contrary, become manipulative and dramatic themselves, attracting individuals with whom they repeat these patterns.
There are also those who, faced with this fear of rejection and loneliness, prefer to isolate themselves and

avoid relationships. However, even in these cases, there is underlying guilt and resentment, as they know that their shadow comes to light in their relationships.

The challenge posed by Pluto in House VII is to learn to look at those wounds of rejection and abandonment that underlie this obsessive attachment. They must understand that relationships are not about controlling, but about facing one's own fears and transforming.

Only by releasing that control and need for security, will they be able to allow their partners and friends to be free, and at the same time, find that freedom and autonomy in themselves. It is a deep healing process that will allow you to establish healthier and more balanced bonds.

In summary, attachment to relationships and intense bonds is one of the main challenges posed by Pluto in House VII. Overcoming it involves a journey of introspection and acceptance of one's own loneliness and vulnerability, to be able to connect with others from a more authentic and liberating place.

Face the fear of rejection and loneliness

One of the key challenges posed by Pluto in House VII of the birth chart is the need to face the deep fear of rejection and loneliness.

As explained, people with this Pluto positioning have a compulsion to be with others, to have friends and partners. They can't stand the idea of being alone, feeling that their security and sense of identity depend entirely on connection with others.

There is an intensity and total dedication in the bonds they establish, where the relationship becomes a matter of "life or death." They can develop very strong patterns of drama and emotional dependency, both in their family and relationship relationships.

However, this obsessive attachment to relationships hides a primordial fear of rejection and abandonment. These people know that their shadow, their darkest aspects, come out in relationships, and they fear that if they are seen as they are, they will be rejected and left aside.

Some of them, faced with this fear, prefer to isolate themselves and avoid relationships. But even in these cases, there is underlying guilt and resentment, knowing that by avoiding attachments, they are also depriving themselves of the chance to heal those wounds.

The challenge lies in these people being able to face this fear of rejection and loneliness. They must understand that relationships are not about controlling, but about transforming and growing. Only by releasing that control and need for security, will they be able to allow their partners and friends to be free, and at the same time, find that freedom and autonomy in themselves.

It is a deep healing process that will allow them to establish healthier and more balanced bonds, where they can show themselves as they are, without fear of being abandoned or rejected. Only then can they find the true connection and security they long for.

In summary, facing the fear of rejection and loneliness is one of the main challenges posed by Pluto in House VII. Overcoming it involves a journey of introspection, acceptance of one's own vulnerability and openness to establishing more authentic and liberating relationships.

Pluto in House VIII

Attachment to power, the occult and transformation

When Pluto is located in House VIII of the birth chart, the person's main attachment focuses on power, the occult and transformation.

As explained, people with this positioning of Pluto usually have an obsessive attachment to control and satisfying their desires. There is an urgent need for everything they want to be fulfilled, and they will suffer intensely when something, whether small or big, does not happen as expected.

These people are described as very powerful, it is even mentioned that in past lives they have probably been magicians or witches, given their strong connection with the esoteric, the invisible and magic. They have great intuition and the ability to read others, and can be excellent therapists.

However, the problem is that, despite this power, they tend to use it more to control and satisfy their own desires than to generate personal and spiritual transformation. There is a tendency to manipulate others and relationships, in order to get what they want.

The challenge that Pluto poses in House VIII is for these people to realize that it is their own obsessions and desires that limit them in life. They must learn to release that control and use their tools of power, not to dominate others, but to transform themselves.

This involves a process of deep introspection, where they can recognize and accept their own shadow, that dark part that they sometimes try to keep hidden. Only by integrating these most unknown aspects will you be able to release your true transformative potential, at the service of your personal and spiritual evolution.

Let go of control and obsession with satisfying desires

One of the main challenges that Pluto poses in House VIII of the birth chart is the need to let go of control and the obsession with satisfying one's own desires.

As explained, people with this positioning of Pluto usually have an obsessive attachment to control and the fulfillment of their desires. There is an urgent need for everything they want to be fulfilled, and they will suffer intensely when something, whether small or big, does not happen as expected.

These people are described as very powerful, with a strong connection with the esoteric, the invisible and magic. They have great intuition and the ability to read others, and can be excellent therapists.

However, the problem is that, despite this power, they tend to use it more to control and satisfy their own desires than to generate personal and spiritual transformation. There is a tendency to manipulate others and relationships, in order to get what they want.

The challenge that Pluto poses in House VIII is for these people to realize that it is their own obsessions and desires that limit them in life. They must learn to release that control and use their tools of power, not to dominate others, but to transform themselves.

This involves a process of deep introspection, where they can recognize and accept their own shadow, that dark part that they sometimes try to keep hidden. Only by integrating these most unknown aspects will you be able to release your true transformative potential, at the service of your personal and spiritual evolution.

In summary, letting go of control and the obsession with satisfying one's desires is one of the main challenges posed by Pluto in House VIII. Overcoming it requires a journey of self-knowledge, acceptance of one's own shadow and learning to use power in a more conscious and liberating way.

Pluto in House IX

Attachment to ideologies and beliefs

When Pluto is located in House IX of the birth chart, one of the person's main attachments focuses on ideologies, beliefs and spiritual visions.

People with this Pluto positioning tend to develop a strong fanaticism for some type of religion, philosophy, or ideological movement. There is a tendency to become very attached to a certain way of thinking, believing and interpreting reality.

This obsessive attachment to ideologies is usually accompanied by great intolerance towards those who think differently. These people have difficulty listening to and understanding those who hold beliefs different from their own, as they hold firmly to their "truth" and are not willing to question it.

Unless the person has other astrological elements that compensate for this tendency, such as a good positioning of Mercury, the big problem with Pluto in House IX is precisely this inability to listen to others and open up to different perspectives.

This is because there is a strong attachment to one's own sense of truth and reality. When someone with this positioning of Pluto encounters ideas or beliefs that question their own convictions, they usually enter into a dynamic of counter-argument and staunch defense of their position.

This can lead these people to experience crises of faith and belief, since their great evolutionary purpose is precisely to allow their truths and beliefs to transform and evolve throughout life.

However, the attachment to the known and the familiar is so strong that it is difficult for them to let go of these preconceived ideas, even when it is evident that they no longer serve them or have weak points. They prefer to cling to them, rather than open themselves to uncertainty and transformation.

Develop tolerance and openness to evolution

One of the main challenges that Pluto poses in House IX of the birth chart is the need to develop greater tolerance and openness to the evolution of one's own beliefs and worldviews.

People with this Pluto positioning tend to develop a strong attachment and fanaticism to some type of ideology, religion or philosophy. There is a tendency to become very intolerant of those who think differently, clinging firmly to their "truth" and not willing to question it.

The big problem with Pluto in House IX is precisely this inability to listen to others and open up to perspectives other than their own. There is a strong attachment to one's own sense of reality, so when someone with this position encounters ideas that question their convictions, they usually enter into a dynamic of counter-argument and staunch defense of their position.

However, the challenge that Pluto poses in this house is for the person to develop greater tolerance and openness to the evolution of their beliefs. Its great evolutionary purpose is to allow its truths and its ways of understanding the world to transform throughout life, instead of stubbornly clinging to them.
This involves a process of letting go of control and the need for absolute certainties. They must learn to listen to others, to consider perspectives other than their own, and to be willing that their ideas and convictions can change and expand.

If they do not do so, these people run the risk of experiencing a crisis of faith and belief, since their attachment to what is known will prevent them from opening up to the uncertainty and transformation that life proposes to them.

In summary, developing tolerance and openness to the evolution of one's own beliefs and worldviews is one of the main challenges posed by Pluto in the IX House. Overcoming it involves a process of letting go of control, listening to the other and being willing that one's own truths can be transformed along the way.

Pluto in House X

Attachment to success and personal demands

When Pluto is located in House X of the birth chart, the person's main attachment focuses on success, on standing out academically, socially and professionally.

The vast majority of people with this Pluto positioning have an obsessive attachment to achieving success and standing out above others. Failure is seen as something terrible, because they feel that their emotional security is tied to the ability to meet expectations of achievement.

These people tend to be very demanding of themselves, with a gigantic level of self-demand. It is very difficult for them to stop and rest, because they feel great guilt for not constantly producing and standing out.

Additionally, they tend to be quite authoritarian and like to direct others. There is a need to be in control and to impose your way of doing things, criticizing those who do not conform to your standards.

In many cases, this attachment to success and personal demands has its roots in childhood, where one or both parents were very demanding on an academic and social level. The boy or girl ended up associating their emotional security with the ability to meet those expectations.

Thus, these people feel safe when they manage to stand out and succeed, but they live terrified of the possibility of failure, because they fear that this means being rejected and no longer loved.

They must learn to look at the feeling of loneliness and abandonment that underlies this attachment, in order to find true security in themselves, beyond achievements and external recognition.

In summary, the attachment to success and personal demands is one of the main challenges posed by Pluto in House aligned with the essence.

Release the need to stand out and learn to serve

One of the main challenges posed by Pluto in House X of the birth chart is the need to let go of the obsession with standing out and standing out, in order to learn to serve the collective in a more authentic and balanced way.

The vast majority of people with this Pluto positioning have an obsessive attachment to success, to the ability to meet high expectations on an academic, social and professional level. There is a gigantic demand towards themselves, accompanied by great guilt for not constantly producing and standing out.

These people tend to be very authoritarian and like to direct others, as they have an urgent need to be in control and impose their way of doing things. They harshly criticize those who do not conform to their standards of perfection.

They must learn to look at the feeling of loneliness and abandonment that underlies this attachment to achievement, in order to find true security in themselves, beyond external recognition. Only then will they be able to develop a way of expressing their potential that is more aligned with their essence.

There is a group of people with Pluto in House X who, in fact, do the opposite of what is expected. Instead of following the path of social success, they rebel and reject those expectations, because they are very angry with their parents and do not want them to continue bossing them around.

However, even in these cases, the challenge remains the same: letting go of control, the need for power and the obsession to stand out, in order to find a vocation that allows them to serve the collective in a more authentic and liberating way.

Pluto in House XI
The attachment to being different and social exclusion

When Pluto is located in the XI House of the birth chart, one of the person's main attachments focuses on the need to be different, to stand out and not fit in with the rest.

These people tend to have a tendency to constantly focus on others, observing what they don't like or what they think has nothing to do with them. There is an attachment to being the black sheep, to showing oneself as strange or eccentric, as opposed to what they consider "normal" or socially accepted.

Astrology mentions that, in many cases, these painful experiences of exclusion and not being seen or accepted by the group generate great anger and resentment towards those who manage to stand out or fit in more easily.

There is a sense that "they" are the popular ones, the successful ones, while "I" am the ugly duckling, the outcast. This dynamic can lead to developing a strong rejection and distrust of others, as they feel deeply hurt by having been excluded in the past.

However, the attachment to being different can also manifest itself in an opposite way. Some people with Pluto in the 11th House try to overcompensate for their feeling of exclusion, striving to be charming and blend in with others, in order to be accepted.

The problem is that, even in these cases, the person continues to feel alone and different, because deep down they know that they are not being authentic, that they are hiding their true essence.

The challenge that Pluto poses in this house is for the person to transform their friendships and social circle, understanding that they have great power to lead groups and cause a positive impact on the community. However, to do this, you must let go of the resentment and anger that arises from experiences of exclusion.

Only by integrating these darker aspects can you unleash your true potential for leadership and social transformation. Otherwise, hate and the feeling that "everything is wrong" will prevent the changes you want from truly lasting.

Transform resentment and open to acceptance

One of the main challenges posed by Pluto in the 11th House of the birth chart is the need to transform the resentment and anger that arise from experiences of social exclusion, in order to open oneself to being accepted and belonging to a group in a more positive way. authentic.

As explained previously, people with this positioning of Pluto usually have a strong attachment to being different, to standing out and not fitting in with the rest. There is a tendency to constantly focus on others, observing what they don't like or what they think has nothing to do with them.

This dynamic can generate great anger and resentment towards those who manage to stand out or fit in more easily. There is a sense that "they" are the popular ones, the successful ones, while "I" am the ugly duckling, the outcast. This leads to developing a strong rejection and distrust of others.

However, the challenge lies in these people being able to transform those feelings of exclusion and not being accepted. They must understand that, in reality, they have great power to lead groups and have a positive impact on the community.

To do this, you need to let go of the resentment and anger that arises from painful experiences in the past. Only by integrating these darker aspects will they be able to unleash their true potential for leadership and social transformation.

Otherwise, hate and the feeling that "everything is wrong" will prevent the changes they want from truly lasting. They will continue to be trapped in a dynamic of rejection and not feeling part of a group, despite deeply longing to be accepted.

The path of evolution implies, then, a process of healing and openness to belonging to a community, without the need to hide one's own essence. They must learn to trust that they can be seen and valued as they are, without having to stand out for being different.

Pluto in House XII

The attachment to control and the feeling of destruction

Pluto in the 12th house is one of the most complex and challenging placements to understand. The 12th house represents the unconscious, the hidden, what is beyond our conscious control. When Pluto, the planet of transformation and death, is in this house, it confronts us with our greatest fears and feelings of destruction.

The main attachment of people with Pluto in the 12th house is control. They feel an overwhelming need to control everything around them, as if their own survival depended on it. This need for control arises from a deep emotional wound that developed during pregnancy and the first years of life.

Many times, the mother's womb during pregnancy was charged with intense energies, such as pain, hatred, resentment or even loss. The fetus, at its maximum vulnerability, was impregnated with those powerful emotions. This left a deep imprint on his cellular memory, a feeling that something terrible could happen at any moment.

As adults, people with Pluto in the 12th house live in constant fear of destruction, of something terrible happening to them. This leads them to develop obsessive and compulsive behaviors, to think excessively, to have phobias or even psychological disorders. They are terrified of silence and emptiness, because that space is where anguish and the feeling that everything is going to fall apart arises.

To try to control this feeling of lack of control, these people cling to all kinds of external anchors: success, relationships, money, even spirituality. But no matter how much they achieve, they never really feel safe and happy. Life continues to ask you to let go of that control, to surrender to trust.

The evolutionary process with Pluto in the 12th house is to learn to look at that feeling of anguish and lack of control, go inward and work at a deep level, at the level of the unconscious. Therapies such as somatic therapies, holotropic breathing or trauma work can be of great help. The key is that the more they try to control, the more they will lose control. Only when they dare to surrender and trust in life, will they be able to access an inner strength and power that no one can take away from them.

Learn to trust life
and let go of control

When Pluto, the planet of transformation and death, is in the 12th house of the horoscope, it confronts us with our greatest fears and feelings of destruction. This is one of the most challenging and complex positions of Pluto, as it confronts us with the deepest part of our unconscious.

The 12th house represents the hidden, what is beyond our conscious control. For people with Pluto here, this translates into a constant feeling of anguish and lack of control, as if something terrible was going to happen at any moment. This emotional wound developed during pregnancy and the first years of life, when the mother's womb was charged with intense energies such as pain, hatred or resentment.

The fetus, at its maximum vulnerability, was impregnated with those powerful emotions, leaving a deep mark on its cellular memory. As adults, these people live with an overwhelming fear of destruction, of everything falling apart. This leads them to develop obsessive, compulsive behaviors, phobias and even psychological disorders, in a desperate attempt to control the uncontrollable.

However, the evolutionary process with Pluto in the 12th house lies precisely in learning to trust in life, to let go of that control that they are so terrified of losing. The more they try to hold on to control, the more it will slip through their fingers. The key is to look squarely at that feeling of anguish and lack of control, go inward and work at a deep level, at the level of the unconscious.

Therapies such as somatic therapies, holotropic breathing or trauma work can be of great help for these people. They must learn to embrace silence, emptiness and uncertainty, without running away from them. Only in this way will they be able to access an inner strength and power that no one can take away from them.

When you manage to surrender to what life presents to you, without resistance, that is when a profound transformation will emerge. They will no longer rely on external anchors like success, relationships, or spirituality to feel secure. They will have found that confidence in themselves and in the flow of existence, which will allow them to let go of control and embrace life with all its potential.

This is a slow and profound process, full of ups, downs and challenges. But as they advance in it, these people with Pluto in the 12th house will discover a strength and resilience that will surprise them. They will learn to trust in life, to let go of control and to surrender to transformation, becoming agents of change and evolution.

How to face the transit of Pluto without fear

Nothing remains the same, there is nothing fixed, no objects, no relationships, no emotions, no financial situations that remain the same. The person torments themselves by trying to hold on to things remaining a particular way, and Pluto will show where they are afraid.

Pluto will also reveal where the person is not showing up in their own power, where they are allowing others to have power over them. Pluto is all about these power games, often with a desire to control life or manipulate others to get what we want. This is the shadow facet of Pluto.

The important thing is to understand that true power comes from within, not from having power over something. It is a power that can be used to build oneself, without having to do so at the expense of others. In fact, if someone else is getting stronger, it shouldn't be at their own expense.

Pluto leads to extremes, both in our behavior and in our emotional nature. There is often an obsession with individuals, commitments, success or appearance. The most important answer is to try to understand yourself through that. It will be a great opportunity to transform yourself psychologically, emotionally and unconsciously, learning to understand your own shadow.

Even if one intends to transform things according to what he understands needs to be transformed, he will still face problems that he cannot predict or imagine. Therefore, it is important to understand that this transit is not something to be afraid of, but something to fully embrace, understanding that the changes in the world are things that have always been changing, we just didn't pay attention to them before. .

OMEGA TEAM

Astrological Souls in Creative Union.
" We explore the inner cosmos and share the wisdom of the stars collaboratively and without ego. Our books are bridges of light in the firmament of knowledge."

Printed in Great Britain
by Amazon